Other Collections by Cheryl Seely Savage:

Give Me a Fragment:
*Glimpses into Motherhood,
Depression, and Hope*

Praise for
Give Me a Fragment:
*Glimpses into Motherhood,
Depression, and Hope*

"A beautiful little book... I was very touched
and recognized the feelings so brilliantly conveyed."

--**Jane Clayson Johnson**, award-winning journalist
with *The Early Show* on CBS, public speaker,
and best-selling author of *I Am a Mother* and *Silent Souls Weeping*

✂ ✂

"This is a short but powerful read. There is everything here that one looks for in poetry, including a variety of styles and cadences. The author's reflections on mental illness, motherhood, and marriage are achingly accurate, as well. As a married mother in a house full of mood disorders, every word resonated with me. At the same time, these are words that are relatable to any and all of us, regardless of our circumstances. There is a longing expressed in these words, one that we all feel; the longing to know, without doubt, that we are worthy.

This is a treasure you will read again and again."

--**Heidi Ashworth**, award-winning and best-selling author
of the *Miss Delacourt* and *The Lord Trevelin Mystery* series

✂ ✂

"This is a beautiful, thoughtful, inspired collection of poetry.
I will be reading and re-reading these!"

--**Alyssa Morris**, award-winning musician, composer,
and professor of music at Kansas State University

✂ ✂

"Cheryl does an incredible job capturing the depth and emotions of a mother. No matter what your circumstance is, every mother can relate to the emotions in between the pages of this book. There is pain, there is joy and there is complete vulnerability in the words of her beautiful poetry.

It is a must read, for sure!"

--**Chalese Stevens**, author, entrepreneur,
and founder of *The Rainy Days Foundation*

Carve a Place for Me

Poetry

by Cheryl Seely Savage

For Molly –

Much Love,

Cheryl S Savage

Carve a Place for Me

Copyright © 2020 by Cheryl Seely Savage

All rights reserved.

First paperback edition November 2020

Book design using Canva by the author

ISBN 9798571194457 (paperback)

Dedication

For Brandon
who lovingly carved a permanent place for me in his heart

Table of Contents

Nature — 1

    The Place Where I Wander *(for Wendy)* — 3
    Spring Snow — 4
    The Death of the Tulip Tree — 5
    Rain — 6
    Leaps Into Her Sky — 7
    Memory of Smell — 8
    Before — 9
    Kansas Floods — 10
    Mirrors — 11
    Someone Like Me — 12
    Carve a Place for Me — 13

Romance and Marriage — 15

    Love Like Austen — 17
    You Will Hear Me Call for You — 18
    Hopeless Romantic — 19
    Thirteen — 20
    Two Souls — 21
    Kiss Me — 22
    Teen Bride — 23
    Wedding Day — 24
    Imagine the Old Ladies — 25
    Remind Me, Again — 26
    Twenty Years — 27
    Tres Leches Cake — 28
    Pilgrimage: A Narrative — 29

Motherhood — 35

    Aching Regret — 37

God in Utero	38
If I Had Known	39
If I Could *(for Nicole)*	40
You Can Always Come Home	41
Where Have All the Good Men Gone?	42
To My Sons	43
Six Decades from Now	44
Nobody Wins the Mommy Wars	45
Those Memories are You	46
My Mother *(for Karen)*	47
For Ashley	48
Catalyst *(for Melissa)*	49
Eternity	50
Inside My Mind	**51**
Sometimes	53
Honestly	54
Melancholy	55
Relentless	56
Faith	57
Sip My Tea	58
Telegram	59
Do Not be Fearful of a Crying Face	60
Dreams	61
When Irrational Stood Me Up	62
Blueberry Pie	63
Glances	64
Good Intentions	65
We Do Not Fit	66
Depression in Two Parts	67
I Was Heard	68

Senseless	69
Where Does That Leave Us?	70
Hiking	71
Wilderness	72
Failure	73
It's Fine	74
Growth	75
How Love is Lost	76
Bitterness, in Four	77
Addendum	**79**
When the Neighbor Stole Our Cat	81
The Only Thing I Hate About Kansas	82
Dreaming, Again	83
Thoughts and Prayers *(for my Muslim and Jewish friends)*	84
Kansas	85
About the Author	87

Nature

The Place Where I Wander *(for Wendy)*
(2019)

Inky ice slaves away
the caterwauling of each broken day
and within the storms that leave behind a dust
of crystallizing diamond shore
I walk
and walk
and walk some more
without a thought except for breath
each tangled worry drops aside
as frozen breathing warms each step
I give it all!
all away
and give it to the frozen day
I want the bulbs, the trees, the dew
the frozen ponds and trails, too
fill me up
breathe cutting air
remove all painful piercing lies
that show up when I realize
how I hear the coyote howling loud
and rustling restless moving sound
before the sun melts rainbowed ice
I float inside the grasses twice
crunching footprints, fall to my knees
but I keep walking down then up
for every step heats my filtered cup
so over and under and wandering far
the trees exhale a solid part—
a hope directly (here
under these ribs)
into my heart

Spring Snow
(2019)

Winter is so silent

It seems odd, twisting branches
Hiding and not expressing
The biting pain that must accompany
When such wet freeze rips to
The bone

We see the beauty and feel the
Softness from our windows and
Allow the world to hover in ice
Because what else can we do?

The Death of the Tulip Tree
(2019)

Twisted branches, gnarled and old
Reach downward, sideways, left-ways, bold
They creak on rested hinges laid
Anticipate the breaking made

And when they drop with crash and pain
Suspended figures, cold refrain
Which cancels nested birds in flight
Eliminates each pinked delight

Then all is silent, shock turns numb
The years it took to grow succumb
To merely fuel for houses, fire
Human's weakness, false desire

Youthful buds, attractive shade
Cycled lives past rivers wade...
Perhaps it's less the death that stings
But more the loss of birded wings

Rain

(2019)

What does it signify when
Giddy, bubbling joy derives from
Pouring, perfect petrichor?
Glowing sunshine satiates but
Soon drains and dries.
Rain; I awaken, stretching, as it
Quenches every thirsty dream.

Leaps Into Her Sky
(2019)

I once saw a bird leap
Which made me stop because
Birds spread wings and fly; did it not
Occur to me how they took flight?
A pause
A look
And suddenly they conquer the air.
Except there is a moment
Like a hush
Barely perceptible, which seems
As hesitation—
Looking closely, I know it is a crouch.
She is not wavering
She is gathering energy
And propelling forward
Boldly leaps into her sky.

Memory of Smell
(2019)

If I was to be limited to the memories of smell
I would elaborate for you the brightness of
Sagebrush in the rain
Sun-soaked brows of laughing children
Suburb lawns infused with lilac.
And if there was time, we would travel down
Wind-swept pines, fragmented salt upon
Ocean waves
Yeasty breads rising in homes built before 1932
Brut cologne, I am seventeen
Finesse hairspray, I am being kissed
Peanut butter chocolate is my husband's smile
Inhaling as I crack open second editions found in
Used bookstores— surpassed only by
Fresh-sliced garden onions in my grandmother's kitchen.

Before
(2019)

Across the valley, in moments
Where wildflowers wave
In a delicious breeze
I can see my heart dancing
Remembering
Dreaming of a future place
Which existed before I knew
My own name...
For such a place, such yearnings grow
Until the shape of my soul
Echoes the call of a
Sparrow

Kansas Floods
(2019)

The rains have not ceased since Spring
Plummeting, pummeling
The packed earth has been made
Black with the mud of torrential rivers
When the news reports flooding
We don't even react
It is now as common as tornado threat
Walking in October meadows
He turned to me and in awe
"How can it be so green?"
We forget, sometimes, how grass grows.

Mirrors

(2019)

Fissured sand, a perfect sheen
Connects too thin the
One, the other;
Glistening silence in
Open-mouthed laughter
Shame in heat, in watchful,
In conscious cover --
In shadow, accidentally
By scraped off, muted
Clouds

Someone Like Me
(2020)

I walk in open spaces
Where there is enough room for
Someone like me
The grass rolls as I pass
Such marked deference and respect
Never fails to lift my head
Flowers do not pass judgment on
My weight, my fears, my politics
The sunrise meets me face to face
Smiling as an old friend
All past wrongs forgotten, for this is a
New day
Mediocrity means nothing amongst
So much beauty— here, in all element,
They are not weeds!
Inhaling unpolluted air I can almost imagine
In this expansive, endless sky
Cradled by ever-changing cosmos
There is still room enough for
Someone like me

Carve a Place for Me
(2020)

Carve a place for me
In wildwood
Where sinew stretching
Lilac-scented wood oak gleams

Sculpt a place for me
On saltwater
Where eyes searching
Coral-painted bright scales sing

Paint a place for me
Above pasture
Where toes pressing
Packed-earth grass buds sheen

Write a place for me
Near cliff-face
Where arms embracing
Wind-swept molded fissures ring

Romance and Marriage

Love Like Austen

(2020)

Adoration is what I wanted
But I received love, instead

We clamor for Byron and Keats
Yet Austen taught us Knightley and Darcy
Words mean nothing if not followed by
Action
And this is why she gave us Brandon

I married not just Brandon,
But Darcy and Knightley and Tilney and Wentworth
Men of purpose, who find the words only when they
Matter

Give me roses and poetry, yes
But carry and push me
Lift and teach me
Remind me what love is underneath, for
I am learning, as Marianne, where true
Romance exists

You Will Hear Me Call for You
(2019)

Maybe when the wind starts blowing
Frothy whites of ships stop mooring
Carefree lowered storm clouds flowing
You will hear me call for you

Maybe when all birds are flying
Forest floors in flowered lining
Roses, ivy, forward climbing
You will hear me call for you

Maybe after friends are leaving
Carried heartache starts retreating
Filtered pretense keeps deceiving
You will hear me call for you

Hopeless Romantic

(2019)

Ferry wind, a joke
But the closest I had been to
Romantic boat scenes
Awkward
It matched most of
Sixteen because I recognized
Laughing eyes
I carry them in my pocket
Praying a string will
Pull loose and so the next time
I peek, they will be
Lost

Thirteen
(2019)

When I first observed romantic love
The real kind, not playground tag, I was
Thirteen
And so overcome my heart would not
Stop sobbing and the embarrassing tears
Running, trailing, forming
A canyon inside of me that filled
To the brim with longing
An urgency to feel it— this! This...

What is this kind of love?
The love from dreams; desperation
For someone to love me
Love me
Love me whole
It wasn't the kiss that moved me
Nor the carefully composed score...

No, I was overwhelmed by the choice he made
By taking her hand
His acceptance
Devotion
Thirteen and I recognized immediately
How loyalty burned lust and
Left it lifeless as dust
Thirteen and I felt bridges slam down
One side and then the other
Crossing the jaded-infested torrents below
To exclaim, "I am in this forever!"

Thirteen and I never cowered
I had witnessed a fictional connection
That purposefully mirrored the possibility and
I never (never!) allowed for less...
Now, turned forty, I thank thirteen.

Two Souls
(2019)

I did not want the other half of my soul
Because it wasn't missing
I needed edges to cut away
My fears
Energy to inch me forward
A forgiving heart for when I am overcome
And when I say we are meant for each other
I infer that my heart recognized, in yours,
How our broken pieces fit—
Melted over, melded around to
Create such a beautiful newness that my
Old soul sighed… and found
A home.

Kiss Me

(2020)

Stop my mouth with
Baited breath
And pull from me my
Insecurity
As gently as you hold my face
Cradle my heart
Wrap my body into the safety of
Your arms...
How can it be, with eyes
Closed and words
Silent, that we can
See and understand
So easily?
Kiss me, love — this space of
Ours is everything

Teen Bride

(2020)

I was nineteen
Different from fourteen when I first
Loved a boy and still different from
Sixteen when I first
Kissed a boy and still different from
Eighteen when I first
Wanted to marry a boy and it was different
Because unlike
Fourteen, sixteen, and eighteen
I saw past nineteen and glimpsed into
Thirty and fifty and seventy-five

Wedding Day

(2020)

I don't remember wanting
Daffodils or roses
Echoes of green, shimmering along
Verdant paths with oaks and aspens
I was focused only on you

I don't remember the cold
How sleet mixed with mud
And snow fell occasionally amongst
Icy paths where we shivered and posed
I was focused only on you

I don't remember the stress
Of selfish guests along with
Low funds, generous loved ones
With cakes, turkey, and cover-up for my nerves
I was focused only on you

I don't remember the details
Conversations with cousins
Eating and laughing and watching
My grandmother dance with my brother
I was focused only on you

I do remember your smile
The tears in your eyes
How carefully you held me as we danced
And the way you gazed at my face—
You were focused only on me

Imagine the Old Ladies
(2020)

Imagine the old ladies with
Dyed hair and wrinkled hands
Laughing, taking photos and wondering
If two so young could make it even
Five years (let alone eternity)
But because they did, these widows
Still in love with their husbands,
They hugged me tight
Told him to cherish me
Ate the cake, signed the book, gave a card,
And sighed deeply, remembering when
They set off for a new life
Hand-in-hand with the kind of love
They ache for nearly every day.

Remind Me, Again

(2019)

Tell me, again, love
How your thoughts turned to me
And what it was that
Adjusted your steps to follow mine.
Was it my smile?
Tell me how you decided your
Heart would ache without mine
And what I said that startled you
From stasis.
Tell me, always again, and remind
My portion of this fusion
When it was that your passion ignited,
Never to burn out, but precariously
Sustain such a life as ours...
Was it my laugh?

Twenty Years
(2019)

It is a marked privilege to age
Alongside someone who
Sees all of your flaws
Understands all of your baggage
Remembers all of your pain
And chooses to love you

Tres Leches Cake

(2020)

The day we packed up to leave California
I cried into the Tres Leches cake
Not because we were leaving but
I had spent four weeks packing
Three weeks cleaning
Two weeks praying
One week falling behind
And as we pulled away, I spilled the cake
The milks didn't run far, but it broke the dam
And I cried, bitterly
He soothed my worry and took us to dinner and my
Sighs and cries were tempered with his
Teasing and carefully placed compassion
He was right about needing a
Detour—we waved to the truck and drove to
Yosemite, our glorious farewell before turning East...
We ate the Tres Leches along the way
Had anything tasted so optimistic?
Had any view been so majestic?

Whenever I see Tres Leches on a menu
I am always tempted.

Pilgrimage: A Narrative

(Gratitude to Jane Austen and her legacy, who influenced my own love story)
(2019)

The pilgrimage began boldly
Flying, alone, business class only
And the Atlantic stretched into blends
Of grey— where do the clouds touch the water?
I worried about swelling; such an elderly
Concern, but I drank water as fast as the
Man in 48G drank coffee
(The alcohol was reserved for the woman in 47A)
Landing, I carefully followed instructions
And laughed when he held up my name on a sign, as if
He was privileged for my presence— didn't the flowers signify?
Kissing, right there, in crowded Heathrow
I could hear the director wanting a replay
But we had trains to catch.

When he told me about London (in England?)
I was angry
Instantly frustrated that he, insistently tropical but remembering he loved
Fish and chips
Was asked to work in London, my London,
My oft-dreamed-for city with youthful fantasies…
Rewind to dewey eyes and affinities for
Green meadows—oh, those accents!
It would be decades until technology
Confirmed what I knew; my blood was thick with it.

It was justifiably unjust
Ten days he would roam where I dreamed
To wander; tattered pages of Austen
Bleached on my fingertips and
Keats held my heart to his lips while I blushed furiously
Under Donne's gaze.
Screenplay adaptations fueled the Anglo-obsession with
Silver lined stories laced with consumption
I only balked at the temptation for corsets
(Ancient Britain, yes, but let's not be hasty
With undergarments!)

It could not be helped, the phrases of Jane
Leapt from Pemberly and stained impressionable blue
I would not yield—
Truth: such conviction led me to find him
I understood, significantly, of character and lust
It did not take seasons to prove faithful love

Once— pay attention— mere months into our measured domesticity,
I pushed the first video cassette into the small
Newlywed approved television set
Scoffing, he watched Mrs. Bennett flit to and fro
Darcy gave Lizzie the cut, directly
And the story— you see, it was the story—
Grabbed a hold of my novice companion
(Austen for the day!)
It would be hours until he slept.

And now, time and budgeted adulthood later
He would sense, smell, see, seep into the
Air of ancestors
He was to lilt and traverse back to familial beginnings
Madness!
He doesn't even adore beautiful, muted petrichor.
Good man, chagrined as he left (I was bereft...)
And as he returned, his eyes
Betraying what my soul already knew: yes, it was the
Dream,
Nothing wanting.
"I will get you there," he said, all prose and promise.

They needed him back, he would have to go
For longer— weeks! coupled with the anniversary of
Aluminum
Ten years together, newly expecting number five
Much can happen in a decade of devotion
This time (do not tease!) he was (it is true!) including me!
I was to come to him; we would celebrate
Together where my yearnings gathered—
Is this possible? I blinked again and again and
Let me see the dates, again!
Yes, please, could you watch our children?
He left while I wrote schedules and updated documents.

He had to work for three days; I put the flowers in water
And took in Kensington.
Using a map, Oyster, and minding the gap
I wandered, alone, amongst millions
History breathed before me, every footstep finding
A path
And crossing the Thames, criss-cross
Swathing through Tower and Cathedral
Could Shakespeare hear my muted exclamations?

Queens and Kings and jeweled cacophony
Sent my soul skyward
I soared there, untouched in Hyde Park
In silence at Elizabeth I
Above such rushing, dear Lioned Trafalgar
Giddiness at Buckingham, Big Ben laughing at
My average reactions; how like a tourist
He could see my wonder and follow my misty eyes
Glancing up... nobody stares at the ceiling for so long.

Do not tell me, local shop worker, that my
Inability to detect cockney equals American stupidity
(I wasn't even upset)
I pay for West End tickets; where would you be without
Wallets and swoons of Anglophile women?

He rented a car; two years in Australia taught him
Left over right
We sped out of the city as I recovered— this, be wary, is the
Suffering part: three days without sufficient water
Naive, naive
Babies need water; why was all the water carbonated?
Ask for tap, no free water to be found
I know --I traversed the tube for a public toilet!
Blessed dehydration slowly abated and we drove
West
Westward to find her
She was non-negotiable, how could I come and
So rudely snub the woman who began my affair—
Wouldn't she know?

But first: homage to the ancients
Towering stones in blasts of bitingly cold
Such frigid wind and I questioned January
Untouched earth, centuries of thoughtful strength
—It was smaller than we thought it would be—
Hydration returned; had my prayers
Been heard by druids or fairies, long-buried
Celts, a whisper of their DNA, pulsing, pounding
(Frenetically drumming)
Inside my connected heart?

Then off across vast countryside of meadowed dreams
Villages, greens, churches unseen
Round and round
My nerves, tingling with anticipation, chewing my
Fingernails, pinching myself
I asked if he knew (yes, he knew!) until we turned into the village
Parked
And dumbfoundedly, we had 30 minutes.

The first time I read Austen, I cried
When I read another, I cheered and found
What it was my soul groaned in sleep
Feelings had thought and thoughts had words
And when words form and follow and finagle through
Content possibly caters— can you imagine?— to change
What of Darcy, what of Ann? Crafted by her mastery
They changed
These weather-worn imaginations
Her characters turned into movie profits and
May have been lauded up for
Cheap dollar fodder, but they were home to me
It did not matter if I was average, typical, plainly
Jane-in-Love as many of my demographic—
Scholars agreed on her brilliance, men have bowed to her
Plotting and building— has not her name withstood time, itself?
I was not ashamed; I needed to see and to feel
To breathe in...
Staring at the door of her home, the place where she lived
And wrote and dreamed and declined, I was
Relieved we were not too late!

Museum workers gave us 45 minutes
We wandered quickly, silently, respectfully as others passed
It was simple, surprisingly normal, a woman
Lived once between four walls, wrote her quilled stories and
Pondering, I do not imagine she ever foresaw her
Small, small, it-really-is-rather-small writing desk
As Mecca, Jerusalem, Golgotha... a shrine to her
Wit, her intimate world.
If she could have observed that room would she have felt
Mortification or aggrandization at such parades of
Numberless admirers?

Perhaps she expected it all

I sighed, and winced, and wished for more
Knowing, he sat beside me in the garden, purchases by my side
And with darkness descending
Pulled out Northanger Abbey (not to be discounted!)
Bent down
Dipped his finger into the fresh, cold, rain-packed earth
And swiped it on the title page.
Grinning at my surprise: "You now have a part of her."

Shall I tell you the closing scene?
The hotel entrance, putting my luggage in the
Black hackney as it rained (such a postcard)
Kissing, kissing, it will only be a few more days
And driving off, always looking back

The seats around me were empty
I curled up, the pilot announcing our ascent
I dreamt about cold wind, black coats, fish, Chawton,
And him
Always him
And settled into a sigh because some of our
Stories have happy endings (it's allowed)
Jane Austen saw to it.

Motherhood

Aching Regret

(2019)

The day I discovered I wasn't me
Came amidst the scared eyes of
My three-year-old son
Evident to many, blinded to me,
I jumped through burning hoops
Meant for paint-plastered performers and not for
Honor-hoarding housewives
I returned to myself amidst the chaos of
Ant piles and soiled flatware
It took a tiny army of pincer-teeth
Before I laughed and shook it all away...
My son learned empathy, but
The past remains.

God in Utero
(2019)

I am overcome.
We created the fleshy shelter
Which houses this divine soul and
Life flows through me
Milky white
To feed this god whose
Ancient spirit is awaiting
Experience, agency, love-which-consumes
And for a moment, a small, small
Did-it-happen moment,
I am his source of everything.
To need me! To rely on such
Imperfection as a compass—
Here, my son! This is the way...
Please do not lose courage
The loud voices are the desperate ones
The quiet voice is from your Mother
The gentle whisper is from your Father
The breeze upon your cheek is from
Realms beyond the memory...
Let me hold you for a while
Let me feed and comfort your heart.
Soon enough I will stand in awe at
Your majesty.

If I Had Known
(2019)

If my younger self knew of the
Difficulty, I would have balked.
It was the not-knowing which
Gave me courage to yield
To the shadowed path of my dreams.
What a relief!
The difficulty has carefully created
Immovable purpose and the
Years have molded into
Lump-in-the-throat joy.
Would it mean so much if it were easy?

If I Could *(for Nicole)*

(2019)

And if I could, love
I would stop and paint
Each step of your precarious journey
With salt (for eating)
Chopin (for soothing)
Autumn (for wonder)
But I have to content myself with
Simply praying that for each
Pebble lodged in your feet
There is a steady branch ready to lift you
Above every consuming boulder

You Can Always Come Home

(2019)

There isn't a reason that can
Prevent us from opening our arms
And folding you back into our hearts
If ever there comes a time
You find yourself wandering (or running)
Limping (or sprinting)
Back to the door of home.
Do not hesitate
No need to knock
Open the door and let peace
Envelop and settle and sigh.

Where Have All the Good Men Gone?

(2019)

Where have all the good men gone?
They are not seen in public view
On television
Being arrested in newspapers
Gossip around the water coolers

What is there to gossip about?
Good men are working, feeding their
Responsibilities, holding the hands of their children
Loving their wives

What is there to be arrested?
Good men are teaching, laughing at
Antics of silly children and wiping away
The tears of their wives

What is there to be reported?
Good men are not causing injustice
But speaking out against it and calling
Down the men who make us all ask

Where have all the good men gone?

To My Sons
(2019)

The tugging will be relentless, son.
Scraping, desperate, howlings will
Disguise themselves as success
And apathy will dress as
Joy — do not walk!
Sprint
Go! Go!
Find the truth:
Beauty is underneath (looks plain)
Loyalty is action (appears busy)
Respect is space (seems so very, very boring)
It is simple to confuse flattery with
Reality and trust sincerity but, son,
Strong men (and wasn't He the strongest?)
Are the gentlest of all.

Six Decades from Now

(2019)

Sometimes it is absolute drudgery
And when I hear "I don't want to just survive, let me thrive!"
I cry
Because sometimes that is the
Face of love
How can we expect miraculous change
In these meme-cliché moments
(I'm a seed, I'm in a cocoon, I'm climbing mountains)
If we abhor the mundane?
Don't pepper me with flowery
Self-affirmations if it will cost me
My sacrifice
I'm earning the secrets of my
Foremothers
They aren't found on social media
In self-help books
In my therapist's office
I find them when I wash another dish
Soothe another cry
Carry a child's whispered hope.
I am being pulled from what
Changes me the most...
And this is when I ask
"Pass me the time, please; show
Me six decades from now."

Nobody Wins the Mommy Wars
(2019)

If forced, I would enumerate
Lists of thousands
Clipped voice, gesticulation
Here are the words I have memorized:
"Still, not good enough."

Taken to bed by seductive
Hairbrush license, watching
False walls click into place
While I hide the axe;
Shaking palms hesitate too long

I could wrench open the window
Ply rusty nails with
Bleeding fingertips, salty
Pooling into a bruise so purple
Moors quake with jealousy (not the wind)

My perspective is a dragon
Only twenty-four heads creeping
Open razor jaws and toothbrush
Bristling; can you not feel the
Fractions peel back my skin?

Exposed so freely, I forget
I am afraid of nudity
Army exposition leads like
Roadkill mourning; I watch the scrubbed
Sink swallow all my questions

Those Memories are You

(2020)

I will not remember every detail
(This should never measure love)
Memory can slip
Time robs us as we focus
On present things
But I promise I will always know
How it felt, the first time, to see you
Hold you, feed you
The relief and joy, indescribable,
Was the same— even when it was different—
How can I know if I cannot remember?
Every day, when I see your face
My heart recognizes the same feelings...
Those feelings are my memories
Those memories are you

My Mother *(for Karen)*
(2019)

She taught several hundred (maybe thousand?) second grade children
Her dedication was evident; many remember her
Some still know her name
We would wake early (read scripture, pray) and we ate
Cold cereal --it had to be quick.
Mom would leave, dad would leave, we would all leave
School days were devoted outside; summer was reprieve.
Never do I remember doubting except
Twice.
I was eleven years old (perhaps twelve) and brimming with
Incriminating self-doubt I wasn't sure
I asked --tears spilled out, ran down my cheeks into my ears as I lay on my bed--
"Do you love me?" I have never seen such shock, such concern, such repentance.
I learned I need words
She learned to give them

I was fifteen (such an age) and knew everything
As I yelled and yelled and slammed the doors
While she yelled and yelled and probably sighing
Maybe while crying
Because here I am, the other end, sighing and crying
My children slam doors. We all yell.
Mothers are not immune to childish things and it occurred to me --
Big love doesn't require big words or big gestures
Only big dedication

Thousands (hundreds?) of second graders adored my dedicated mother
She loved them, served them
But her big love was for her children
She doesn't remember all of those names
She prays to God for mine, often.

For Ashley

(2019)

Brace yourself, daughter
For this frightening world
Is far lovelier than
Even the kaleidoscope
Inside your dreams

Catalyst *(for Melissa)*
(2019)

She was a catalyst for healing
As she grew inside of me
The darkness lost all room
And vacated, although slowly

Her light was far too loud
And her song was far too bright
For negativity to keep winning

It was as if every prayer
I had uttered until that time
Was manifested within her tiny body

Her soul was so
Big it took over our space
And I gladly allowed it to
Give the darkness ejection orders

Eternity
(2019)

Do not tell me I've missed out on life
Haven't lived
Should have taken the time to find myself
Because what did I miss?

Undisturbed flesh, blood-shot eyes
Nights filled with daytime regret
Confusion and focus on Franklin
Allowing time to rob harvests and
When they flee, it cannot be found, again.

Do not tell me I have lost all time
I am not old
Accomplishment does not cease to end
This side of 25; and what will be my gratitude
When I become old and am left alone
With whispers of memory?

Death will not take from me my unpopular choices
Fear of missing out cannot touch me.
I will last forever and experience it all because
My legacy will permeate illusions
Through the living.

Do not tell me sacrifice, service, sensitivity
Attaches me to fools.
Giving it my all looks like giving it all away
But who can sense what is in my heart and
How it expands exponentially?

Do not tell me I have not lived
That I have not been found
For I lived every day and
Was never lost from the beginning.

Inside My Mind

Sometimes

(2019)

Sometimes it leaps out of me
As if I were a dragon
Belching fire and death
Uncontrolled and consuming

Sometimes it is a joke
Where the buildup fails
Flatter than the punchline
That doesn't make any sense

Sometimes it pulls me under
Like weights on ankles and
I see the light fade as the
Waves gently move above me

Sometimes I mistake it for normal
As a hangnail or mosquito bite
Annoying and festering but not
Cruel enough for noticing

Honestly

(2019)

Lazy, grazing, resting eyes
Lift up thyselves and realize
That even while they circumscribe
Truth rarely poses compromise

Nothing gained from inner lies
Can sweep away the valor sighs
And wasted years of soiled skies
Leave dusted, broken diatribes

Stand among the olden why
Be careful of restrained goodbyes
Seek for more than bloodline ties
Beyond the scope where mortals rise

Melancholy

(2019)

When I want melancholy
I simply turn inward and pluck it
From the origin
And when I want giddiness
I also grasp inside
Fumble about until I latch
On, and without apology
Wrench it free

Relentless

(2019)

They will attempt breakage
So don't scoff when they approach
Because you will not be as prepared
As you insist in your
Repetitious journals.

The ache is relentless and the
Haunting greets so politely— confidently
Rehearsed, but the smile doesn't reach
Your ears.

Listen!

It isn't your dreams and yearnings
Which make you pale
It is the inordinate stagnation
At the ignorance of time.

Until you have seen the sloping deepen
Do not assume you are simply too tall;
Plunge down, immerse! And carefully slow
Your breathing.

Inhale the vistas
Rewrite the road
Delve the roots and wave the branches
And laugh when they come to your door.

Faith
(2019)

I looked over, spread about
The lofty frantic tears
And when I set myself inside
I realized those fears

Were set upon the tabled guilt
And rung from gabled shores
The shaded light revealed the root
Which gathered stinging lore

Did we know such suns were there?
Did we seek their face?
A whisper, gentle by my ear—
I turn, expect embrace

But disappearing in the mist
A hand, it beckons me
I'm left with moments shroud in faith
To follow and be free.

Sip My Tea

(2019)

If I took away only one part
Of this oiled, dress rehearsal life
Perhaps you could understand
But you cannot mirror
Any but your own
And this is why I have learned
To ignore the barking
And sip my tea

Telegram

(2019)

If I could have a telegram office
Lodged in my ear, with instructions
For when confused or annoyed
Maybe my words
Wouldn't seem so ignorant
To the people who only
Know me through occasional
Public appearances
Although, I am reminded
Those who know me best
Often misunderstand as quickly
As the internet trolls:

We are all navel gazers
We are all truth grazers.

Do Not be Fearful of a Crying Face

(2019)

Do not be fearful of a crying face
The presence of tears signifies
Water in the well
Be afraid of the dusty eye
When crying is done
Cannot be sung
Chalky dust leaping up from
A well so dry, clawing at it
Only reverberates unbreathable air

Dreams

(2019)

The last time I remembered my dreams
In a vivid, flowing fashion
I was so depressed that my life
Could not pull me forward like the nightly REM
I wanted to sleep and sleep and sleep
Not just for reprieve from reality
But so I could live in the fantasy
Where inadequacy couldn't haunt me
And fortitude gave me gallantry

It's been more than a decade since
I skewered the glowering beast
And dragged him under the bed
But sometimes when dark episodes hit me
I will reach for my pillow and ache to remain
How incredible! Dreams are now shadows
They are weak, full of plot holes
I finally awoke! And life pulls
Me back to all of my heart's goals

There is little I want in a fake world—
I am building my truth in the real one.

When Irrational Stood Me Up
(2019)

Curtains parted, Sense peeked out
Watching for her long-awaited visitor
The cushions had been vacuumed
Tea was on the table
Even the hand soap in the bathroom smelled
Of vanilla (or maybe coconut?)
She watched and waited, pressed palms
Down the sides of her pressed skirt
Glanced — again— at the clock
When the tea was cold and the cucumber
Went limp (was the bread too light?), she
Finally sighed, left her her heels by the locked door
And quietly went up to bed
It was not the first time Irrational forgot
To call and cancel

Blueberry Pie
(2019)

I once made a pie, blueberry
It leaked all over the counter, dripping
Underneath the cooling rack, rising
Steam above the gooey crust
And I wasn't sure where I went wrong
Embarrassed (again, as I do not cook often
Or well),
I read the recipe as I scooped up
Blue, heated soup
There it was... cornstarch. How did I forget?
It seems I'm always forgetting and
Leaking and
Scooping

Glances

(2019)

An upward glance—

I mistook the pressing sordid oak
While learning subterfuge
And there idyllic ivy hung
Green and bursting rain deluge

Be careful, voice; open
Mouth under eaves is often
Cause of drowning

They claim all-the-things
To stop a boring song
Mirrors take and crack the side
Where lungs and heart belong

I don't mind...
I may glance sideways.

Good Intentions

(2020)

Pity, this, a concluded
Convoluted entrapment where
Words betray before they leap
From my fingertips
Initially poised to soothe, forge, fuse
Until they snapped, stopped— take
A moment and realize what we see:
Stretched-over with sinews
Exposed, the scraped, bleeding muscles...
"Please avert your eyes while I
Wrestle..."
Fisted— I close my eyes
Swallow
Bear the heated shame
Why didn't they tell me? Feeling
This much, pockets of
Implosions, pothole-filled
Explosions, does it even matter
I have good intentions every moment?

We Do Not Fit

(2020)

We do not fit
Like jigsaw pieces
Into every face, ideation, relationship
Effort does not always yield
Acceptance
For some, mistakes create
Beautiful arrangements of forgiveness
Others prefer to walk away
From smoldering ashes...
I mourn the ash
Walk away
Focus on where I fit
But look over my shoulder and wonder
If pieces change over time and are
Allowed to try, again

Depression in Two Parts
(2020)

Part two is the reminder
Of ice-melt, it leaks
From crevices cracked from fissure
Because the length of the shame
Burrows into the sinew

Part one was the fire, melting
Apart metallic enclosures which
Seemed secure and now drip
Molten and dry into weak-crusted
Canopies

It never holds together
For long

I Was Heard

(2020)

And when I went over the wall
I sensed the secret of my garden wasn't
Simply Flora or Fauna
I had to seek it, study it, wrap it, love it...
Microscopic engrams floated in the
Cottonwood air
Hazy filters erased thorn-bushed pockets
Pressed against my waiting palms
It seemed to me I would tarry endlessly
Removing vine and lifting leaf
Dissecting pools of silver water
Singing movement, dancing cadences
Drawing unfinished lists in muddied rock
My prayers were uttered in starlight, flecks of
Flint, emblazoned across an inky sky
And I was heard

Senseless
(2020)

What do you mean,
"It makes no sense?"
It exists by such definition
Because if it "made sense"
The solution would be easy
Sensibility isn't the question;
Ask yourself
"Is there pain?"

It never asks permission
Before eroding what makes sense
It never sought approval
Before taking up residence
Eradicate it without remorse— it
Spares none for you

Where Does That Leave Us?
(2020)

If I let down my hair
They will notice and if the mascara
Streaks, perhaps they will see
But granting an open palm is
The only muted way to eliminate the
Softened blow; let the
Water flow where it goes
Rocks cannot edge backward
And where does that leave us?

Hiking

(2020)

When I was eighteen and the hike
Seemed steeper and higher than I
Remembered at ten but I knew the
Next bend would take us to the
Last part but it did not and neither
Did the next and it kept going and
Climbing without any care as the mountains
Laughed because it took them
Millions of years to learn how to settle and sit
So still and I'm always overwhelmed and
Sometimes I stop and rest too long in
Protest because the Mountain isn't
Going back in time to change the
Route and lessen the curves and make my
Hike less demanding and forgetting how
Strain sometimes leads to the
Very best views

Wilderness

(2020)

I once read a book
About the overpowering loneliness of
Wilderness and Frost described the
Desert in the soul
But I never understood
Until I stopped being glue
And waited for
Whatever it was I hoped to
Happen and with mortification
Realized I was a commodity

Don't pretend our roles are
Anything more than a placation
Vacation

Perhaps I'll move to Alaska?

Failure

(2020)

Precarious precipice
Taunting with promises of vistas
How many times must I plummet
Until I keep behind the
Guardrail?

It's Fine

(2020)

As if steel wool scraped
Waxed wood, the words
Feed at the edges of my mind
Rough, excruciatingly numbing
And I blink, "Pardon me, can you repeat the
Question?"
She asks how I am doing, even
As she begins to move away...
"Tired. Tired, but... good..."
It was exactly as rehearsed, and
Satisfied, we both flee before either of us can
Admit the hours we need to clean out
Hidden trash and gunk and awkward
Sobbings we reserve for the shower.
It's fine, friend, fine!
We will do our
Spring cleaning another time

Growth

(2019)

Every seed must forgive
Every flower for not
Adequately alleviating the
Pain of growth
Gasp and stretch through the soil
Fumble and push to the light—
It is the same for all—
Bitter, exhilarating, can-I-do-this process
Resulting in stunning beauty.

How Love is Lost

(2019)

One after another they fall
Blazoned with mocking yellow
Blowing over broken street lamps
Rushing, rushing as if late
Shaking branches, pretending nonchalance
Such cowardice paints affectation
And they agree, as one, to turn away
This is how love is lost
It isn't crumbled or dusted
It simply rolls away and forgets
Refusing opportunity to amend
No backward glances
Excruciating farce laced with regret

Bitterness, in Four

(2019)

1.
"Be unique," I read, "be bold, too!"
But what they really mean is
"Don't be you."

2.
Addictive loneliness insists on
Spinning cobwebs and inordinate cocoons; such
Empty shells I toil to fill without any
Substance beyond disappointed yearnings. Still—
Ravenous, I feast on the broken promises and
Gorge myself on empty courage; but
When the sun comes up I notice
My loneliness is of my own making.

3.
Pickled, plastered, pointed white
Shouldered, strapping, scorching light
Huddled, harried, hungry blight
Freckled, festered, floating might
Carried, cradled, careful flight
Mourning, muddled, mangled sight
Begging, bumbled, bleeding right
Riddled, reigning, resigned fight

4.
Periphery wonder placed
In my palm
I close my aching fingers
Kiss my fist

Addendum

When the Neighbor Stole Our Cat
(2019)

Quite into a fray

Testing our trust in humanity
We almost felt sorry for her
Until the military husband lied to the
Police we resolutely had to call

And!

She pulled out a shotgun

It was a level of insane my
Depressed, diseased brain
Could not recognize and so
We imagine he still lives there.

Perhaps he's happy?

The Only Thing I Hate About Kansas
(2019)

Kansas is a lovely place
It has my heart, no lie
But man, the bugs, they're everywhere!
I'm happy when they die

Ticks, mosquitos, orbing webs
Cicadas, beetles, too...
Have you heard of chiggers, no?
I hope you never do!

There are ants and flies, assassin bugs
Bagworms on the trees
Be careful where you sleep at night
There's even lice and fleas!

So, welcome Fall, you glorious thing!
And bring in Winter's chill
I'll miss the Summer in the cold
But bugs? I never will!

Dreaming, Again

(2020)

I long for the days when my dreams were believed
And wonder was met with applause
Before life's unyielding critical gaze
Stepped in to point out all my flaws

In youth we have nothing to tell us our dreams
Are mad or impossibly met
They stretch out before us as beautiful hope—
We haven't yet lived in regret

I wonder, in earnest, if I can dream them, again
And reach for impossible stars
To leave behind failings and words tainted bleak
To be more than a lifetime of scars

Thoughts and Prayers *(for my Muslim and Jewish friends)*
(2019)

Small sphere of influence means
There is not much beyond
Thoughts (how do they feel? What can I do?) and
Prayers (pleading for comfort, community, caring).

Conversation on computer chips
Rarely change opinion
Although I try; I pass along
Information and purposely
Compose rational thought.

But I continue to give
Thoughts (what were their names? How can I
Honor them?) and
Prayers (please protect, prevent, prepare)

Doing something is better (action!)
I am told over and over and over…
Believe me! I agree; landlocked in a
Community where most nod and shake
Their heads in mutual horror.

And we keep giving
Thoughts (can I donate? Sign my name?) and
Prayers (but by Grace, not us, not us)

I turn to my children and
Gently implore them to seek
For goodness; even as the world
Around them becomes the living
Reality of all nightmares.

For this, I will always give
Thoughts (send peace, live in peace, create peace) and
Prayers (give us love, help us love, here is my love)

Kansas

(2019)

Breathing prairie
Enough to hold all the secrets of every
Pioneer hope and dream.

The wind carries the
Smell of caressed grass, flowing waves
Grown with fresh sunshine.

They call to me
These giants of green and earth; the
Homes of beast and fowl

And reflect the
Moving sky, where blue and white
Connect heaven to home.

About the Author

Cheryl Seely Savage was born to Canadian parents and raised in southeastern Idaho. She has a Bachelor's degree in Family Studies, eight children, and is married to her favorite person. When she isn't writing poetry, she is teaching piano lessons, reading novels, managing chaos, planning dream vacations, conquering depression, and practicing her faith. Cheryl and her family currently reside in the Flint Hills of Kansas.

Carve a Place for Me is her second poetry collection.

Made in the USA
Monee, IL
08 December 2020